ESSENTIAL DK COMPUTERS

MULTIMEDIA

PLAYING MUSIC ON YOUR PC

D0967080

ABOUT THIS BOOK

Playing Music On Your PC is an easy-to-follow guide that
explains how an ordinary home computer can be used to find
and then play back different kinds of music.

THE PERSONAL COMPUTER HAS MADE A
remarkable transformation from a
mere business tool to a flexible
and powerful home entertainment system.
One of the key factors in this development
is its ability to store and play back hi-fi
quality music.

This book explores the different ways in
which a home PC can be used to play
music, whether it's an audio disc from
your CD collection, or a free digital song
that you've downloaded from the Internet.
It explains how it all works, how to play
audio CDs, where to find free digital
music, how to download it, and all about
the player programs that you will need to
enjoy the music.

Along the way, we'll explain a little about
the different audio formats you're likely to
come across, as well as looking at their
most important characteristics. Starting
from scratch, we'll
tell you how to
find Sonique –
one of the
best music

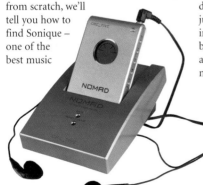

playing programs around – and provide
step-by-step instructions explaining how
to download it, install it, and use it to play
music. We'll also show you how to have
fun customizing Sonique so you can adapt
its look and feel to suit your own personal
sense of style.

For anyone who likes to take their music
with them, there's a section on portable
digital music players, which can be used
just like a personal stereo. However, the
important difference is that they can also
be connected to your personal computer
and then ingeniously enable you to copy
music back and forth.

By the end of the book, you'll have a
clear idea of the musical capabilities
of your PC, as well as information
and guidance on where to look
on the Internet to find sites that
offer music files that you can
download and then play for free.

ESSENTIAL DK COMPUTERS

MULTIMEDIA

PLAYING MUSIC ON YOUR PC

ROB BEATTIE

A Dorling Kindersley Book

Dorling Kindersley
LONDON, NEW YORK, SYDNEY, DELHI,
PARIS, MUNICH, and JOHANNESBURG

Produced for Dorling Kindersley Limited by
Design Revolution, Queens Park Villa,
30 West Drive, Brighton, East Sussex BN2 2GE

EDITORIAL DIRECTOR Ian Whitelaw
SENIOR DESIGNER Andy Ashdown
PROJECT EDITOR John Watson
DESIGNER Andrew Easton

MANAGING ART EDITOR Nigel Duffield
SENIOR EDITOR Mary Lindsay
DTP DESIGNER Jason Little
PRODUCTION CONTROLLER Wendy Penn

Published in the United States by Dorling Kindersley Publishing, Inc.
95 Madison Avenue, New York, New York, 10016

First American Edition, 2000

2 4 6 8 10 9 7 5 3 1

Copyright © 2000 Dorling Kindersley Limited
Text copyright © 2000 Dorling Kindersley Limited

Published in Great Britain by Dorling Kindersley.

A catalog record is available from the Library of Congress.

ISBN 0-7894-6372-5

Color reproduced by First Impressions, London
Printed in Italy by Graphicom

For our complete
catalog visit
www.dk.com

CONTENTS

MUSIC ON THE PC

PCs are now capable of displaying moving pictures and playing CD-quality music. This chapter explains how to find music on your PC and outlines the key formats you'll encounter.

THE MULTIMEDIA PC

A typical home PC now has hundreds of times the memory and thousands of times the storage capacity of early computers. High-resolution color screens allow PCs to display full-color photo images, and computers equipped with DVD drives can play back entire movies. In addition, the cost of PCs has plummeted.

THE KEY COMPONENTS
The four devices to look out for are a sound card, speakers, modem, and either a CD-ROM drive or DVD-ROM drive. Thus equipped, you can play conventional music CDs ⌐, download music from the Internet ⌐ to your computer, organize and catalogue libraries of digital music and, if you have a portable MP3 player ⌐, transfer your music to it.

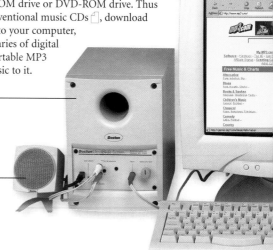

Subwoofer ●
A subwoofer, like the one here, is not always supplied with other speakers, but will improve the overall sound.

Speakers ●
Today's PCs typically feature powered stereo speakers.

WHY YOU NEED A MODEM

A modem connects your PC to the telephone system and then to the Internet where it can "talk" to any other connected computer.

SOUND CARD

The sound card contains the "engine" that allows a PC to play back digital sound at CD-quality. It also stores an entire "orchestra" (e.g., pianos, strings, etc.), which can be used to play back MIDI files ⌐. At the back of the sound card, you'll find connectors for plugging in speakers and a microphone, along with a "line in" socket into which you can plug (and record) instruments.

SPEAKERS

Speaker prices have dropped to the point where a set with a subwoofer – a floor-standing speaker for improved bass – is reasonably affordable. Stereo sound is piped through two satellite speakers placed either side of the monitor (these usually deliver better performance than speakers attached directly to the side of a PC's monitor).

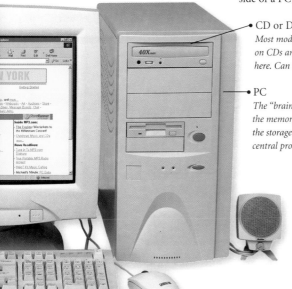

● CD or DVD Drive
Most modern computer programs come on CDs and are loaded onto the PC here. Can also play music CDs.

● PC
The "brains" of the computer – contains the memory needed to run programs, the storage to keep them safe, and the central processor that makes it all work.

Storage
Modern PCs have hard disks capable of storing hundreds of hours of CD-quality music, along with CD or DVD-ROM drives that can play conventional music CDs.

9 **Where the MIDI file format fits in**

AUDIO CDs

You are probably very familiar with using your computer's CD-ROM drive to load the programs that you need, but have you realized that you can also use the CD-ROM drive to play any of your favorite conventional music CDs?

PLAYING AUDIO CDS

Simply place the music CD in as normal (with the label facing up) and you'll be able to listen to it through the speakers that are included with most modern PCs. You'll notice that the front of the CD-ROM drive doesn't have any fancy controls (though it may have a headphone jack and a simple-volume control wheel) but fortunately, Windows includes a free CD playing program that has all of the features of a "real" CD player and – as we'll see later on – a good few more. When you've finished listening to the CD, you can eject it either by using the button on the front of the CD drive or by clicking on the relevant control in Windows' own software CD player.

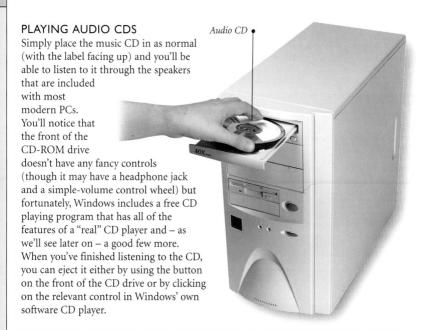

Audio CD

WHAT IF I HAVE A MACINTOSH?

If you own a Macintosh rather than a PC, you can still play lots of sounds, from conventional music CDs through to the most up-to-date MP3 music. You do not have such a wide choice of MP3 players as you would if you were using a PC running Microsoft Windows, but you can find them.

Start with Apple's own QuickTime player (free to download from **www.apple.com/quicktime/**) and keep up to date with Mac music by visiting **www.macrocks.com/audiomidi/index.html**.

MP3 FILES

There are many ways of recording and saving music digitally, and each one generates files with specific characteristics; some are also better at doing certain jobs than others. Currently key formats are WAV, Real Audio, WMA, and MP3.

FAVORITE FORMAT

MP3 is the format that everyone's talking about. It's the most popular way to store and play digital music on the Internet, on ordinary home PCs, and on dedicated personal MP3 players (battery-powered devices much like tiny personal stereos). MP3 has become so popular because, compared with other forms of digital music, it is able to squeeze songs recorded at near-CD quality into files that are around one-twelfth the size of uncompressed audio files.

MP3 Everywhere
You can listen to music as you work, or on the move, with a portable MP3 player.

WHERE THE MIDI FILE FORMAT FITS IN

MIDI is completely different from the other formats here. The others are all ways of storing digital recordings, while MIDI is simply a set of instructions that tells electronic instruments what to play, rather like sheet music telling an orchestra what to play. The instruments are all stored on your PC's sound card, and when you load a MIDI file it contains all the instructions that tell the sound card which instruments and notes to play, how loud, when to start and stop, and so on. Because MIDI files are simply sets of instructions, they are very small.

TINY SIZE – TERRIFIC SOUND

Artists who want to "master" a song onto CD often store their work as a WAV file. However, while the quality of such files is excellent, they are very big. What makes MP3 music so compelling is its ability to deliver close to CD-quality results while taking up very little space. The same song recorded as an MP3 file is a fraction of the size of the WAV file. Yet if you were to play the two files one after the other, you'd hardly be able to tell the difference.

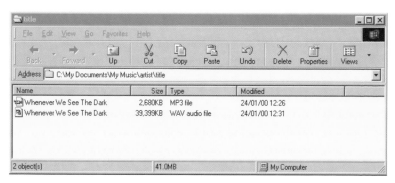

Comparing File Size
Here we can see exactly the same piece of music recorded using two different methods. The top piece of music has been recorded as an MP3 file, and is just over two-and-a-half megabytes in size.

Underneath you can see exactly the same song, but this time it has been recorded as a standard Windows audio file (labeled here as a WAV audio file). At almost 40MB, this file is nearly 15 times larger than the MP3 file.

FLEXIBILITY

MP3 has made it much easier to store large libraries of music on PCs, transmit music over the Internet (smaller file sizes are sent more quickly), and encouraged hardware manufacturers to develop personal MP3 players that can store a CD's worth of songs and yet remain affordable. There is also a wide range of programs that allow you to play MP3 music on your computer, along with those that help you create and compile libraries of music downloaded from the Internet. Such music is widely available and free to download. Keep up to date with new music and what's happening on the MP3 scene by visiting websites such as www.mp3.com.

K-Jöfol
This is a typical MP3 player. Individual tracks can be organized into playlists and you can control the treble and bass with the graphic equalizer.

PORTABILITY

Music on the PC is hardly portable, so to listen to music on the move, you will have to invest in a portable MP3 player. These are tiny, pocket-sized, battery-powered digital personal stereos that store music files in their special solid-state memory banks, or on tiny plug-in memory cards. Like their CD equivalents, MP3 players are highly portable, but because the music is stored digitally in memory – rather than on the surface of a CD – they won't jump if you want to take them jogging or listen to music while riding a bicycle.

In its simplest form, you can use your home PC to play conventional music CDs, just like a traditional hi-fi system, and we'll look at how all that works later. However, the real revolution in modern music surrounds a relatively new way of recording and storing music on your PC in a format called MP3. Music stored like this takes up around one-twelfth of the space that you would normally need to record at CD quality. This results in small files, which makes it perfectly possible for anyone with a modem and a PC to download MP3 music from the Internet.

Portable Player
The size of a portable MP3 player belies the power within. This player can hold almost a full CD's-worth of material.

DO-IT-YOURSELF RECORDING

Remember that with a microphone you can record your own voice on your PC and save the results as a WAV file. Every sound card has a socket at the back and you can plug your microphone into this. Then, using the Windows Sound Recorder program, you can make and save your own simple recordings. To access the program, go to the **Start** menu and then choose **Programs>Accessories> Entertainment**, and then **Sound Recorder**.

DOWNLOADING

If you've never downloaded a file from the Internet, all this may sound daunting, but it isn't. Good websites provide clear, simple instructions (usually of the "click here to begin" variety) on how to start copying the file from where it's stored on the Internet down the telephone line to your computer. Once there, it will typically appear as an icon on your Windows desktop; double-clicking it will start the installation process. From then on, it's just like installing a commercial program from a CD-ROM.

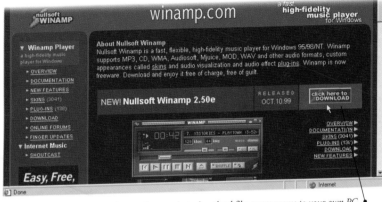

Good websites make it clear what you have to do to download files or programs to your own PC

FINDING MUSIC

You can easily find ready-made MP3 music on the Internet. Modern search engines such as AltaVista (**www.altavista.com**) now help you to search specifically for websites that include images, audio, and video – which makes it easier to track down music sources on the Internet. Of course, as we will see later in this book, there are hundreds of sites dedicated primarily to music that include all kinds of free tracks, player programs, and other interesting material.

GETTING MUSIC TO YOUR PORTABLE MP3 PLAYER

Portable MP3 players come with all you need to get your music from a PC into their memory banks. Typically, this involves connecting the two units with a simple cable and then starting a program on the PC that establishes a link between them, and allows you to examine and edit the contents of the MP3 player, changing play orders, replacing tracks, and so on.

THE WAV FORMAT

Every owner of a Windows PC will already have some sounds stored on their hard disk in the WAV file format. When you switch your computer on in the morning for example, the sound that you hear as Windows starts has been stored as a WAV file – it's called The Microsoft Sound and you'll find it in the folder called Media, inside the Windows folder. If you have a microphone plugged into your sound card and you record the sound of your own voice, it will be saved as a WAV file.

The Windows Sound Recorder program

This displays the sound quality

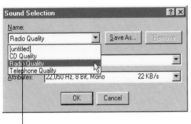

• *Change the quality of the sound here*

TYPES OF WAV FILE

Windows allows you to record three types of WAV file – Telephone Quality, Radio Quality, and CD Quality – and the higher the quality, the larger the file size will be and, as we know, large files take a long time to download from the Internet. The WAV format is therefore very good for making and playing back recordings on a modern PC with lots of hard disk space. However, it is not so good for downloading over the Internet because the file sizes are too large and would take far too long to download.

THE REAL AUDIO FORMAT

Real Audio was the first popular file format to offer "streaming audio." With streaming audio, you never actually download the file – instead you go to wherever it's stored on the Internet and play it from there. Music stored like this begins to play almost immediately after you click on it. However, results can vary enormously depending on the quality of your Internet connection and the amount of Net traffic. Generally, music broadcast using Real Audio is radio rather than CD quality, but the attributes that allow it to be "streamed" make it very useful, especially for listening to radio stations over the Internet or to live concerts.

Here's a list of websites containing Real Audio content

Real Player can also display a "best of" selection of sites containing Real Audio content

WINDOWS MEDIA AUDIO

Something of a newcomer, Windows Media Audio deserves attention for a number of reasons. First, it claims to offer MP3 levels of audio quality but with files that are half the size so they download over a modem more quickly and take up less space on your hard disk. Second, it's claimed to be equally useful for playing complete files stored on your hard disk, or streaming music from the Internet rather like Real Audio. Third, it has the weight of the world's most powerful PC software company behind it – Microsoft. Like Real Audio, Windows Media Audio is just one component of a much larger multimedia program that also handles video, and although it's still not as prevalent as Real Audio, a number of popular websites will offer visitors a choice between the two. Currently however, there are many more websites offering music in MP3 format than in Windows Media Audio format.

Clicking on a song title automatically loads the player program

Windows Media Player playing a file stored on a pop band's website

PLAYING A MUSIC CD

The easiest way to get acquainted with PC music is simply to play one of your CDs in your CD-ROM or DVD-ROM drive. A typical home PC with Windows already includes all you need.

THE WINDOWS CD PLAYER

Sophisticated audio has become a key element for today's home computers. The three devices to look out for are a sound card, a set of speakers, and a CD-ROM or DVD-ROM drive. You will be able to play conventional music CDs, copy tracks from your CD collection to your computer, organize and catalogue libraries of digital music and, transfer your music to a portable MP3 player.

1 OPENING THE DISC DRIVE

● To play a music CD, open your PC's CD-ROM or DVD-ROM drive by pressing the button on the front. When the tray slides out, place the CD with the label facing up and then either press the button again to close it, or gently push the tray back in.

2 LOADING THE PLAYER

● Assuming you haven't fiddled with Windows' default settings for the CD player, it will sense that you've loaded a CD into the drive and go off and check it out. When it recognizes the disc as an audio CD that it can play (as opposed to a CD-ROM containing programs, which it cannot play), then the CD player will load automatically. You don't have to do anything.

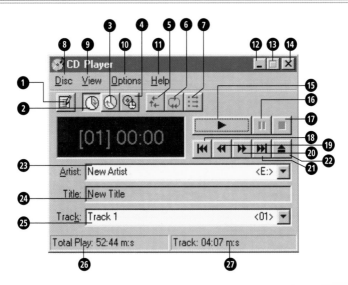

THE WINDOWS MEDIA PLAYER

1 Edit play list
2 Track time elapsed
3 Track time remaining
4 Disc time remaining
5 Random track order
6 Continuous play
7 Play track intro only
8 Access the disc menu
9 Change the look of the CD Player
10 Access different playback options
11 Access the help program
12 Minimize
13 Maximize
14 Close
15 Play
16 Pause
17 Stop
18 Previous track
19 Rewind
20 Fast forward
21 Next track
22 Eject CD
23 Artist name displayed here
24 CD name displayed here
25 Track name displayed here
26 CD length
27 Track length

CD-ROM OR DVD-ROM DRIVE?

It is best to get a DVD-ROM drive because it can do all the things a CD-ROM drive can do (play music CDs, install Windows programs, play games) and in the future, when programmers start to make use of its superior sound, video, and storage capabilities, it will be able to do much more.

3 PLAYING THE CD

● To play the first track of your CD, simply click on the **Play** button on the CD Player. When the song starts, you can use the other controls to pause, stop, rewind, fast forward, or skip between tracks.

Play button ●

CONTROLLING WINDOWS CD PLAYER

The Windows CD Player allows you to type in the name of the artist, the album, and all the track names, so that when you play the CD you can easily jump between favorite tracks, rearrange the order, and so on. Moreover, you only have to key in the

information once. The CD Player software is able to idetify the particular CD, link your data with it, and store the data. The next time you put the CD in to play it, the software recognizes the disc, and loads all the stored information again.

1 START THE PLAYER

● Put a music CD in the CD-ROM drive and close the door. When the CD Player starts, go to the **Disc** menu and choose **Edit Play List**.

2 DISC SETTINGS

● Here, you can see that there are locations for the artist and album name, and also for each of the tracks.

● Currently both the **Play List** and the list of **Available Tracks** just reads **Track 1**, **Track 2**, and so on because their names haven't yet been entered.

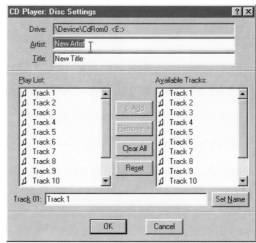

3 ADDING ARTIST/ ALBUM NAMES

● The cursor jumps straight to the Artist name, so just enter it and then press the Tab⇆ key (just above the CapsLock key) to move to the next empty field. Then type in the album name.

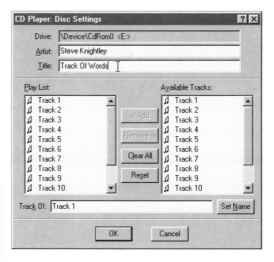

The Tab⇆ *Key*
Pressing the Tab⇆ key moves the cursor forward through the successive text locations (known as "fields") in a dialog box.

4 ADDING THE TRACK NAMES

● Find the text location toward the bottom of the screen with **Track 1** in it. Click the mouse after the **1** and, holding down the mouse button, drag left to highlight **Track 1**.

● With **Track 1** still highlighted, type in the name of the first track. When you've finished, click on the **Set Name** button.

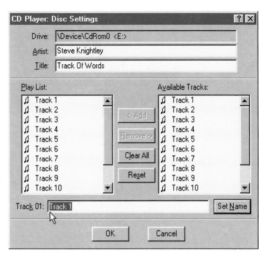

WHAT TO DO IF YOU CAN'T HEAR MUSIC

Check that the speakers are plugged into the correct jack on your sound card, that they are switched on, and that their volume is turned up. Click on the **Start** button and then choose **Programs> Accessories> Entertainment**, and then **Volume Control**. Check that the faders are turned up, and that the **Mute** option of each slider hasn't been accidentally checked.

● The name you type appears at the top of the right-hand column. **Track 2** now appears in the box. Highlight that and type in the real name of track 2. Then repeat for each track.

● Remember to click the **Set Name** button, rather than clicking on the **OK** button. Clicking the **OK** button at any stage will close the dialog box, and we are not ready to do that yet.

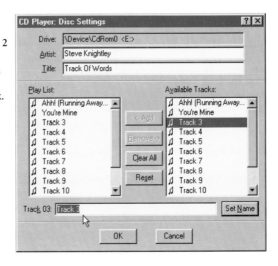

5 UNDERSTANDING PLAY LISTS

● You can now see two columns in the dialog box. On the right is the list of **Available Tracks**, while on the left is the **Play List**. At the moment, the two are identical, and, if you click on the **OK** button and then the **Play** button, the CD will play all the way through from track one to the end.

● Let's say that, having entered all the track names, you only like tracks 1, 2, 3, 4, and 5. You can remove the others from the **Play List** so that they don't play.

● In the **Play List** column, click on track 6. Then scroll down to the end of the list and, while holding down the ⬆Shift key, click on the last track. Tracks 6 to the end are highlighted.

● Click the **Remove** button and they'll disappear from the **Play List**, but not the **Available Tracks** List.

Remove button ●

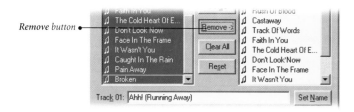

6 CHANGING THE PLAY ORDER

● Open the **Disc Settings** dialog box again 🗋.

● Let's say you want to move track 5 so that it plays ahead of track 1. Click on track 5 and hold down the left mouse button. Two musical notes appear next to the cursor.

19 Disc settings

● Keep holding down the mouse button and drag the track up to the top of the list. You can tell it's being dragged correctly because an arrow appears in the left margin showing that the track is changing position.
● When the track is in position, release the mouse button.
● Click on **OK** to close the dialog box. Your tracks will now play in the new order.

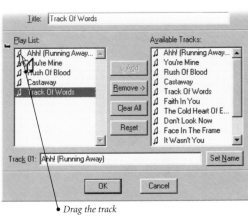

● *Drag the track*

YOUR SOUND CARD IS YOUR FRIEND

PC sound cards are very powerful and you'd do well to find out exactly what yours can do. Make a point of visiting the manufacturer's website (the address will be in the the sound card manual) to check for the latest drivers (small programs that may improve performance), as well as hints and tips.

MP3 PLAYER PROGRAMS

In order to play MP3 music you need a player program. There are many of these and – amazingly – all the good ones are free. Here is a selection to download and use.

THE CHOICE IS YOURS

There are many different MP3 players available for free on the Internet. Each has a slightly different set of features or a slightly different way of implementing them, but all allow you to play and organize high-quality digital music.

SORITONG

Soritong is an MP3 player that is a combination of good looks and powerful organizational features.

Despite its extravagant interface, Soritong has all the player controls of its more conventionally designed cousins, and is admired for its Music Manager module – the part of the program that helps you organize a large number of MP3 files easily. After typing in brief details for each song, you can view your collection in many different ways (sorted by Title/Artist/Album/Genre). You can also make your own playlists quickly and easily.

Like many modern MP3 players, enthusiasts can change the visual "look" of Soritong in all sorts of wild and wonderful ways. In addition, the program features a number of special audio effects, which are fun and include an Equalizer, Crystalizer, Vocal Reducer, Techno Enhancer, and Wide Stereo. This player can be downloaded from **www.sorinara.com**.

MAPLAY 1.2

This was one of the first free MP3 players for Windows and, although its popularity has waned in the face of competition from Winamp, Sonique, and Microsoft's own Windows Media Player, many people like it for the simple, no-fuss interface. It is small, fast, offers good facilities for creating and maintaining playlists, and can be downloaded from **www.mp3now.com**.

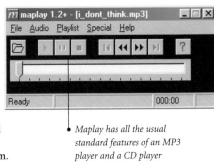

• *Maplay has all the usual standard features of an MP3 player and a CD player*

REALJUKEBOX

RealJukebox lets you create, play, and manage personal collections of digital music in several popular audio formats. Specifically – and alongside MP3 – it allows you to play Real Audio files, one of the most popular formats used on Internet sites for "streaming" music down to home PCs. The quality is not as good

as MP3, and rather than copying the song down to your computer and playing it from there, the song is played directly from the website.

Record companies will often make available Real Audio versions of their artists' songs to promote a new album or a tour. You can download RealJukebox for free from **www.real.com**.

Play •   *Eject* •

Record •

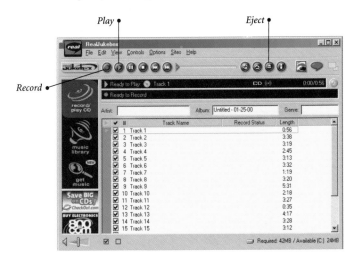

A Typical MP3 Player

We have already had a look at two Windows music players – Windows Media Player and CD Player – but there are many more players to be found on the Internet and, although they differ visually, they perform most of the same functions. Let's now take a look at one of the most popular players – Winamp.

WINAMP

Winamp has become one of the most popular programs available on the Internet because it's very good at what it does. Winamp may be small, but it packs a big punch, and allows you to play not only MP3 music, but also music stored in a variety of different formats. This flexibility makes it especially popular with people who don't want to clog their hard disk with a number of different programs. As with many other downloadable programs, if you don't like the appearance of Winamp, you can customize it by using "skins" that change its appearance without affecting Winamp's functionality. And, as well as changing the look of Winamp, you can add special visual effects that pulsate in time with the music – and they can be great fun.

Winamp has the same controls as a conventional CD player.

By clicking and dragging these sliders with the mouse, you can fine-tune the treble and bass response

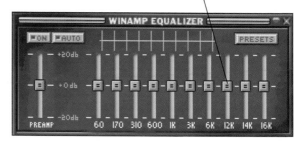

These controls mean that you can customize and then control playlists of your favorite music.

Playing an MP3 file is only part of the story. You need to be able to control the quality of the sound and organize your music into playlists. To that end, players like Winamp offer all of the equalization controls of a conventional stereo as well as the facility to manage libraries of music by combining them into playlists.

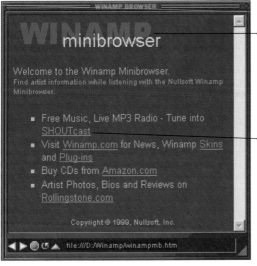

Winamp includes its own tiny web browser, which you can use when you're running the main player program to access Internet sites.

The underlined words are links to websites. Clicking on one of these will connect you to the Internet, using Winamp's minibrowser, and then take you to the website itself.

WHERE CAN I FIND OTHER MP3 PLAYERS?

There are dozens of good programs for playing MP3 music and many of them are free. Try visiting www.askMP3.com and then clicking on the section heading called "MP3 Players." Scroll down the site and you'll find them organized according to the different computers they work with.

DOWNLOADING SONIQUE

We have seen a selection of MP3 players in the previous chapter, but we will now focus on Sonique, one of the best known – and visually most interesting – MP3 players.

FINDING YOUR MP3 MUSIC PLAYER

You can use one of the Internet's search engines (think of them as being a bit like telephone directories of websites) to find an MP3 player or, if you know the address, go straight there. Good sites will contain clear instructions about what to do next.

DOWNLOADING AND INSTALLING
Before you can install an MP3 player, you have to find it on the Internet and download it. Although this may sound complicated it is really very easy, but it does assume you have an operational modem and an account with an Internet service provider. For our screen shots, we'll use Microsoft's Internet Explorer as the browser, though the steps here will work exactly the same if you're using Netscape Navigator or Communicator.

1 CONNECT TO THE INTERNET
● Connect to the Internet in your usual way. Your web browser will load and take you to your home page.

Internet Wisdom
To find out more about the Internet, see *Getting Connected*, *Searching the Internet*, and *Browsing the Web* in this *Essential Computers* series.

2 GETTING TO THE SITE
● Next, type in the web address **www.sonique.com** and hit the [Enter ↵] key on your keyboard.

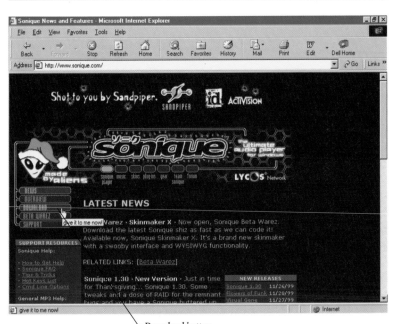

• *Download button*

3 ARRIVING AT THE SITE

● When you arrive at the Sonique site, click once on the green **download** button on the left of the screen.

● This takes you to the next page. Scroll down until you see the green **Download Now** button and click on it.

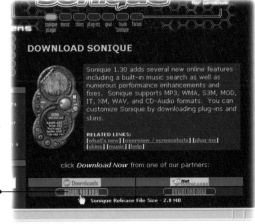

Download Now button •

DOWNLOADING THE MP3 PLAYER

The next task is to download the Sonique MP3 player program. This means copying the files to your computer's hard disk by following the instructions on screen. These change from time to time, but in general they follow the sequence shown here.

1 STARTING TO DOWNLOAD

● On the next page, find and click on **Download Now** – the words are highlighted in blue.

2,935,280 downloads

Download Now button ●

● Wait a moment and then, depending on how your web browser is set up, you may see this dialog box. If you do, click on the **OK** button to save the file to your computer's hard disk. If you don't, skip to the next stage.

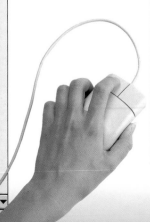

2 CHOOSING THE LOCATION

● Windows then asks you where on your computer you want to save the file. Accept the default by clicking on the **Save** button. Here, we're saving the file to our Windows desktop where it's easy to find.

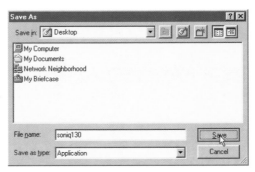

3 LEAVING IT TO DOWNLOAD

● Sit back and relax as the file copies itself onto your computer. This screen will show you the progress being made as the file is downloaded. To ensure that this screen closes when the download is complete, tick the check box.

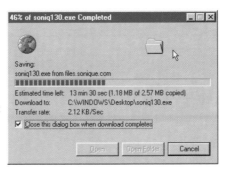

● When it's finished, close your web browser in the usual way and disconnect from the Internet. Our newly downloaded file is on the desktop and is ready to install.

KEEPING YOUR PLACE

So that you don't have to keep typing in long web addresses, web browsers have a feature called *bookmarks* or *favorites*. When you find a website you might want to revisit, tell the browser to add it to a special list. When you want to return to it, click on the name of the website in the list.

INSTALLING THE PLAYER

The next thing to do is to install the Sonique MP3 player onto your hard disk. Once again, this is a very easy task to do and only involves following onscreen instructions. You are now only minutes away from being able to play MP3 songs.

1 STARTING THE PROCESS
● First, make sure you're not running any other programs, then double-click on the Sonique icon to start the installation process.
● When the dialog box appears, click on the **Yes** button.
● Sonique then prepares to install itself.

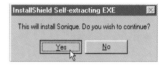

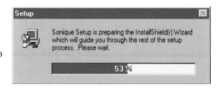

2 THE WELCOME SCREEN
● At the Welcome screen, click the **Next** button once you are certain that you are not running any other programs.

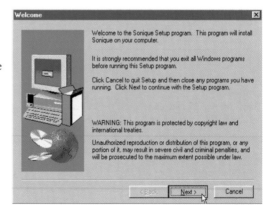

SHAREWARE AND FREEWARE

Shareware is software that works on the honor system. Usually, you download it from a website without charge and then you have the author's permission to try it out for a while. If you like it, you then pay the license fee. If you don't, you should delete the software from your computer. Some shareware programs are deliberately crippled (for example, they won't save files or they stop working after 30 days) so that you can't use them fully without paying for them. Freeware is simply software that is free to use.

3 READING THE AGREEMENT

● Read the license agreement, make sure you agree with it, and then click the **Yes** button. To read the remainder of the text, use the scroll bar at the right of the panel.

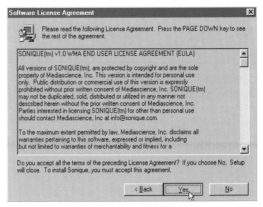

4 CHOOSING THE DIRECTORY

● You can tell Sonique to install to a specific directory, but it's fine to accept the default here by clicking on the **Next** button. If you know what you're doing – and have a specific reason for wanting to install it elsewhere – then click the **Browse** button and follow the instructions that appear.

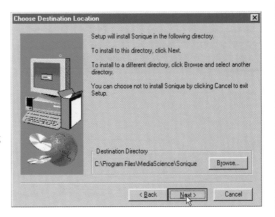

5 CREATING A FOLDER

● Allow Sonique to create its own Program Folder by clicking on the **Next** button, providing that you don't want to give it an alternative name.

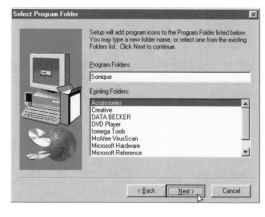

6 STARTING THE INSTALLATION

● Click on the **Next** button to start copying the Sonique files to your computer.

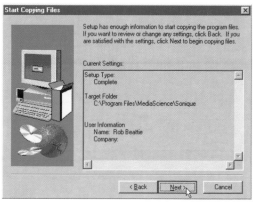

READ CAREFULLY

When you're installing a new program you can usually accept all its suggested defaults, but it does pay to read each dialog box carefully and give some thought to the options you're being offered. If you decide to change your mind about a decision you've made, you should be able to. Most good installation programs will allow you to alter some of the settings – even after the program has been installed.

7 CHECKING THE BOXES

● Make sure there's a check mark in all the boxes on the **Supported File Types** dialog box by clicking inside them. Then click on the **Next** button to continue the installation.

8 INTERNET CONNECTION

● Select the radio button that describes your Internet connection type. If you're at home, it should be the first one – **I connect to the Internet with my modem** – so click inside it to select it and then click on the **Next** button to continue.

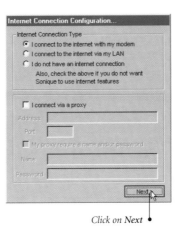

Click on Next ●

WHICH SITE?

How did we know that the player program we wanted was at a website called **www.sonique.com**? The short answer is that we've been there before and kept a note of the address. As you surf the Internet, use search engines, such as AltaVista (**www.altavista.com**) or Yahoo! at: (**www.yahoo.com**), clicking on links, and generally exploring, you start to discover all kinds of interesting places that you want to return to.

9 FINISHING THE INSTALLATION

● Sonique is now installed. Make sure that neither of the boxes in this dialog box, which automatically appears, are checked, and click on the **Finish** button.

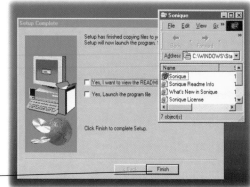

*Click the **Finish** button* •

INTRODUCING SONIQUE

Sonique features a playlist, the ability to handle 12 types of audio files, and it uses very little of your computer's resources.

Recent upgrades include a built-in music search, better performance, and you can download other appearances – or "skins."

1 SONIQUE REVEALED

● Double-click on the **Run Sonique** icon on your desktop to run the program.

Suit yourself...

If you don't want to install a program in its preferred directory, simply click on the **Browse** button. This will then allow you to use Windows file commands to install your new program to another folder on your computer's hard disk.

● A small form appears where you can enter your details and register the program if you wish.

2 SONIQUE'S MANY FACES

● Sonique loads and plays its theme tune.

● One of the interesting and useful aspects of Sonique is that you can display it in three different sizes. Find the words **navigation console** and double-click on them. The player shrinks to the size shown at bottom right.

● Sonique plays its theme tune

*Double-click on the words **Navigation console** to shrink Sonique*

● Move the cursor over Sonique in its new format and you'll see the controls slide into place.

● Sonique at its smallest size

● Change the size again by double clicking on the Sonique logo. It now looks like this.

MULTIFACETED SONIQUE

● You can explore the program more thoroughly for yourself. When you begin using the program you'll discover all kinds of neat functional tricks and little visual surprises. In this view, for example, you'll see that the name of the track being played is displayed in the lower window.

● Check the annotated view of the full-sized Sonique (opposite) to get a complete run-down of all the various buttons and controls. Many of the controls, such as play, pause, jump tracks, and volume, are duplicated in all three of Sonique's views.

● Click the **Help** button for more information – it's labeled with a question mark.

● *The Help button*

THE SONIQUE PLAYER

1. Change size once
2. Change size twice
3. Help
4. Minimize
5. Close program
6. Previous track
7. Next track
8. Pause
9. Play
10. Up (scrolls up through the available visual effects and skins)
11. Down (scrolls down through the available visual effects and skins)
12. Volume
13. Volume boost
14. Balance
15. Pitch
16. Store treble and bass settings
17. Find music-related websites
18. Find and download music
19. Organize music into playlists
20. Sonique's many visual effects view
21. Change settings
22. The program's version number
23. Program credits and other information
24. Graphic equalizer
25. Individual tone slider controls
26. Open music track or playlist
27. Set loop mode
28. Set shuffle mode

ACCESSING MP3 FILES

To play MP3 files, you need to find MP3 sites on the Web, know how to download files to your hard disk, and how to organize them by using playlists – all of which are explained here.

WHERE DO MP3 SONGS COME FROM?

It's all very well to talk about downloading MP3 files from the Internet and playing them on your computer, but where do these files come from in the first place? And who's putting them on the Internet for you to download?

PROMOTIONAL SITES

There are four main kinds of MP3 music sites. First, there are those that promote artists that don't have any kind of record and distribution deal. For example, **www.mp3.com** has become a showcase for acts trying to publicize their music without the aid of a traditional recording contract.

The www.mp3.com site is a good example of a website that promotes less famous artists and groups. As you can see, it's divided into genres so you can find the music you're interested in more easily. The site also makes it very clear that the music is free to download.

MUSIC INDUSTRY SITES

Second, there are those sites that work in conjunction with record companies to promote their artists in various ways. Music magazines with a web presence do this, along with sites that concentrate on specific genres of popular music. Then, there are reference sites such as the Ultimate Band List (**www.ubl.com**), which also incorporates lots of MP3 music for you to download and play. This music has been properly contributed by the artist involved, their record company, or their management team.

Here we've logged on to the Ultimate Band List website (www.ubl.com) – a sort of online encyclopedia of popular music with discographies, biographies, and a good selection of downloadable MP3 files.

MORE MP3 SITES – BRIEFLY

www.dimensionmusic.com As well as music, this site is an MP3 community with news, forums, and chat.
www.2look4.com This search engine doesn't return dead sites – it checks indexed sites every 30 minutes.
www.listen.com A directory-based search engine that monitors thousands of sites and offers music reviews.
www.mp3.org The ultimate site about all things MP3.

ARTISTS' SITES

Third, you'll find that established artists will often place MP3 files on their websites and allow you to download them legally.

You might, for example, discover a bonus track on the site in MP3 format that's not available on the released CD; artists and groups sometimes put a song from a forthcoming album on their websites early so fans can get a taste, or they might put excerpts from the album on the site, and so on. Whatever the approach, they're happy to use MP3 music as part of a mix of promotional activities.

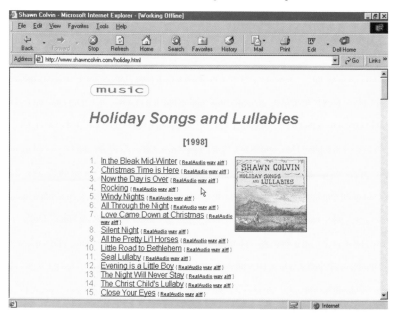

For those sites that do not wish to use the MP3 format, possibly due to fear of digital piracy, Real Audio is a popular choice, as seen above.

WHAT DOES THE RECORD INDUSTRY THINK OF MP3?

Naturally, the record industry is very concerned about the piracy issues. To that end, they've been working on a way of digitally "watermarking" MP3 recordings with an authorization code. Illegal recordings without the code simply won't play. This is called the Secure Digital Music Initiative, or SDMI.

WAREZ SITES

Finally, there are the so-called "warez" sites, which occupy the seedier end of the Internet and are full of illegally copied and illegally distributed MP3 files. These should be avoided.

THE REAL AUDIO ALTERNATIVE

The recording industry prefers the Real Audio format, firstly because its quality isn't good enough to make it an alternative to buying a real CD, and secondly because, as you never actually download a Real Audio file, pirate copies cannot be made.

DOWNLOADING AN MP3 FILE

In this section we will tell you how to find a typical MP3 song by searching on the Internet, how to download it, and then how to play it using the various features included in any web browser and in the Sonique MP3 player program.

1 FINDING THE SONG

● Start your web browser. When you arrive at your start page (ours is **www.altavista.com**), find the Address line under the button bar.

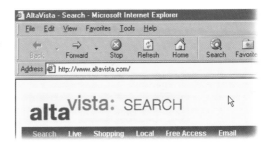

● Click on the address to highlight it and then type in **www.mp3.com**.

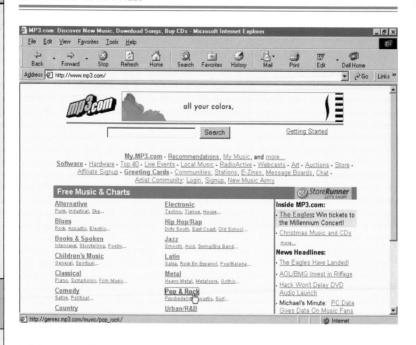

● When you arrive at the MP3.com website, find the **Pop & Rock** category and click on it.

● When you visit, the number one song will have changed, but the principle of what you do next is exactly the same. Click on the name of the number one song (it will be underlined).

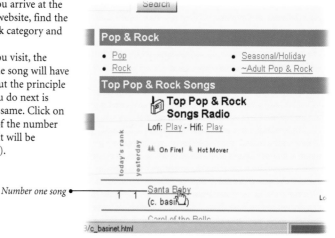

Number one song ●

2 DOWNLOADING THE SONG

● Here, you're taken to the song itself. Find the word **Download**. It will be highlighted in some way, perhaps in red, or underlined in blue. Click on it.

Santa Baby   Seasonal/Holiday
Lo Fi: Play (28.8k modems or faster)
Hi Fi: Play (high-speed connections)
Download (3.1 MB)
Song Lyrics & Story   Email Song   Save to i-drive
Description: Just a tiny wish list for Christmas. Please see "artist's Calendar and notes". Happy Holidays and a joyous millineum's end. Peace, cynthia.

MP3

● **MP3.com** then asks for your email address. Type it in the space provided and then click on the **Continue Download** button.
● The song (**Santa Baby** in this case) is then copied from the website to your hard disk.

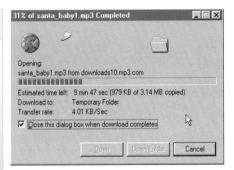

Enter Email Address

Welcome to **MP3.com**. To help us personalize your experience, and deliver periodic news on your favorite music, new site features, free music CDs, and other general announcements, please enter your full Email address below.

You'll only be asked once for your email address as long as you use the same computer and have cookies turned on.

Email Address [youremail@email.com]

(If you are concerned about giving us your email address, please read our Privacy Policy)

Continue Download button ●

    Continue Download

AUDITION YOUR MP3 SONG FIRST

Good websites store their music in formats other than MP3. Look out for those that use Real Audio or any other streaming audio format because they start playing straight away, so you can listen to a song to find out if you like it before downloading it.

31% of santa_baby1.mp3 Completed   _ □ ✕

Opening:
santa_baby1.mp3 from downloads10.mp3.com
■■■■■■■■■■■■■■■
Estimated time left: 9 min 47 sec (979 KB of 3.14 MB copied)
Download to: Temporary Folder
Transfer rate: 4.01 KB/Sec
☑ Close this dialog box when download completes

   Open   Open Folder   Cancel

● When the download is completed, Sonique loads automatically and begins to play the track.

MAKING A PLAYLIST

Before you can play MP3 music, you need to find it on your computer, and then tell Sonique where it is. Once this has been done, you can begin to compile a playlist and start enjoying your chosen music whenever you wish.

1 FINDING MP3 FILES
● Load Sonique by double clicking on its icon, then make sure that you're using the largest of its three views.

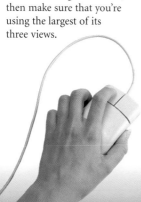

● Next, click anywhere on
the Windows desktop and
then press the F3 key. The
search function appears.
● In the **Named:** box, type
in ***.mp3**.
● Find the **Look in:** box,
then click the downward
pointing arrow. From the
drop-down menu, click
once on the **(C:)** drive icon.

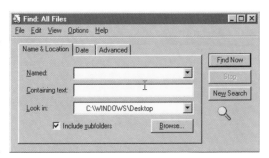

Named box ●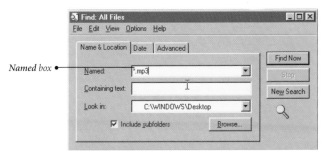

OPENING SONIQUE QUICKLY

There is a shortcut that
you can use to open
Sonique. Move your
mouse cursor down to
the Windows taskbar
(the gray strip along the
bottom of the screen)
and click on the mini
Sonique icon to the
right. A menu appears
that lets you start the
program, and offers you
your most recently
played songs.

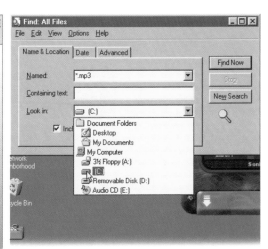

● Click the **Find Now**
button. Windows goes
off and finds all the files
with an MP3 suffix – no
matter where they are on
your computer.
● When the list of found
files appears, click on the
name of the song you
downloaded (again, **Santa
Baby** in this case).

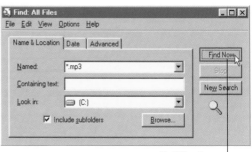

Find Now button ●

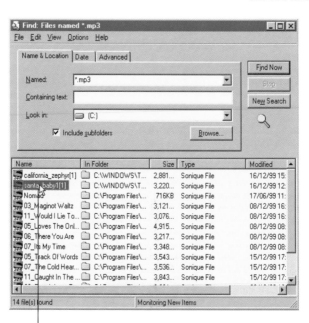

● *This is the song that was downloaded*

● With the song title highlighted, click on it and, holding down the mouse button, drag the cursor across the screen from the Find box to Sonique. As you hover over Sonique, two extra icons are added to your cursor – an open rectangle and a plus sign to indicate that the file is being copied. When you see these, simply release the mouse button and the song will begin to play.

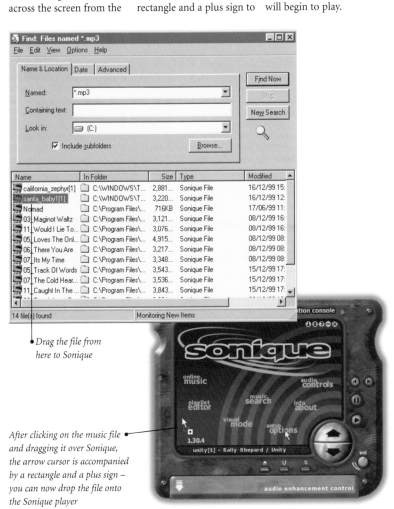

Drag the file from here to Sonique

After clicking on the music file and dragging it over Sonique, the arrow cursor is accompanied by a rectangle and a plus sign – you can now drop the file onto the Sonique player

TAKING CONTROL OF YOUR MUSIC

Sonique provides some excellent controls for cataloguing and then organizing your MP3 music in various ways. It's never been so easy to create customized playlists of your favorite music so that it plays according to your preferences.

1 MANAGING PLAYLISTS

● Add a few extra tracks in the same way – download three tracks from the Web, and drag them into Sonique. Then click on the words **playlist editor**.

● Your three songs will appear. Obviously, their titles will be different from these, but they'll look the same in the list and behave in the same way.

● Click on **sort** and you can arrange your list of songs into alphabetical order. Alternatively, **shuffle** plays them in random order, while **reverse** and **clear** perform precisely what they say.

Playlist editor

Your three songs

● You will probably want to use the playlist that you have created again. If you do, click the **save** button.

Sort button ●

AVOIDING ILLEGAL MP3 SONGS

If you stick to the official sites of the artists and their record companies, you can be sure that anything there respects the relevant copyrights of their creators and publishers. However, some sites constructed by fans may not, and you should use these with caution. The real piracy villains, however, usually signpost their intentions pretty brazenly and are to be found in the same electronic neighborhoods as the obviously phony get-rich-quick schemes and pornography sites.

Save button ●

● When the dialog box opens, the word **untitled** is highlighted to indicate that you can type in a name for your playlist.

● In this instance, type **acoustic list** in the box and click on the **Save** button.

● To prove it's been saved, click the **Clear** button and the tracks will disappear from the list.

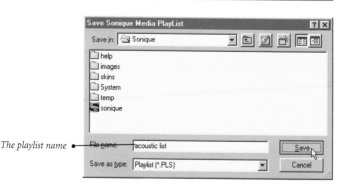

The playlist name ●

The Clear button ●

● Now click the **Open** button to open the dialog box on screen.

The Open button ●

● When the dialog box appears, find your playlist (called **acoustic list** here), and double-click on it.

Find the playlist that you want to hear ●

● The playlist loads and the first song immediately starts to play.

MUSIC ON THE MOVE

It's OK having digital music available on your computer, but how do you listen when you're away from it? For this you need a portable digital music player, known as an MP3 player.

THE PLAYER

MP3 players have been around in one form or another for a few years now, but it was only really in the course of 1999 that they started to become very popular. Until then, they had been too expensive and suffered from having too little memory.

FLEXIBLE AND PORTABLE

Now, however, MP3 players offer more memory, an expansion slot, better controls, and easier-to-use software – in general – delivering high-quality music at an acceptable price.

Although individual models differ slightly in what they can do – and how they do it,

MP3 players share many of the same functional and physical features and they come with similar programs to help you transfer your music from the computer to the player. However, although it's clear that the MP3 format is very exciting, it still has some way to go before it can match the flexibility of the compact disc.

For example, should you decide to take an MP3 player away on vacation, you will be limited to whatever songs you decide to copy over from your computer – you can't just walk into a store and download new ones – but it is probably only a matter of time before that becomes a regular weekend expedition.

CREATIVE LABS' NOMAD – A TYPICAL MP3 PLAYER

① Headphone jack
② Microphone
③ Play/pause button
④ Stop button
⑤ Next song
⑥ Previous song
⑦ Record voice notes/Erase MP3 files
⑧ LCD displays track information, battery life, and other information.
⑨ Opens memory card compartment
⑩ Volume control
⑪ Switch between music radio and voice recording modes
⑫ Repeat current track/Treble and bass controls
⑬ Locks all controls in current position
⑭ Compartment for rechargeable batteries
⑮ Memory card eject slider
⑯ Door flips up to reveal memory card compartment

CONNECTING THE PORTABLE PLAYER

A portable MP3 player needs to be physically connected to your computer in order for the two to work together properly. Although each player looks slightly different, they all connect, and then work, in more or less the same way.

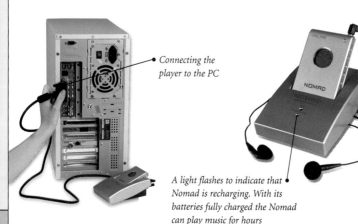

Connecting the player to the PC

A light flashes to indicate that Nomad is recharging. With its batteries fully charged the Nomad can play music for hours

1 LOADING THE SOFTWARE

● Having connected the Nomad, you load the manager software. This then makes a connection with the player in the dock. It then examines and displays the contents of its internal memory.

The PC "talks" to the MP3 player through the connecting cable

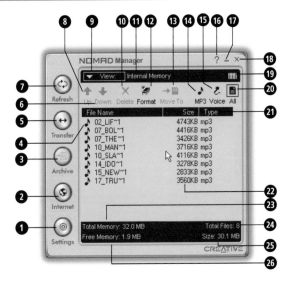

THE NOMAD MANAGER

❶ Settings – fine tunes the PC-to-player link

❷ Internet – takes you to relevant Internet sites

❸ Archive – copies voice notes to your PC

❹ The song list

❺ Transfer – copies songs between player and PC

❻ Down Arrow – moves song down the song list

❼ Refresh – updates the Nomad display

❽ Up Arrow – moves song up the song list

❾ View – views songs stored in the player's memory or on the expansion card

❿ Delete – deletes the current song

⓫ Internal Memory – indicates which part of the player's memory is currently displayed

⓬ Format – wipes everything from the part of the player's memory currently displayed

⓭ Move To – sends selected songs to the PC

⓮ MP3 – display only MP3 files

⓯ Voice – display only recorded voice notes

⓰ Help

⓱ Minimize

⓲ Close

⓳ Display – change the song display

⓴ All – display all files

㉑ Type Column – displays the file type

㉒ Size – displays the size of each song

㉓ Total Memory – total available memory

㉔ Total Files – number of songs stored in the current player view

㉕ Size – how much memory the songs take up

㉖ Free Memory – how much memory is left

2 VIEWING THE MUSIC

● Clicking the **View** button like this allows you to switch between the list of songs on the Nomad's internal memory and those stored on its memory card.

● Clicking the **Transfer** button opens up a window onto your computer. You can see the window on the left displays what's on the Nomad itself, while the window on the right lets you look at what's on your computer.

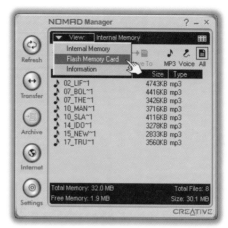

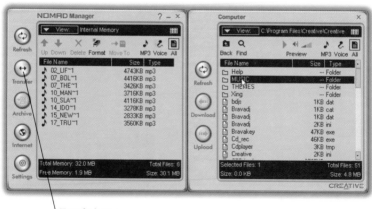

● *Transfer button*

Palmtops
Palmtops can be used to play MP3 files too

PALMTOP COMPUTERS

If you have a palmtop computer that uses Microsoft's Windows CE operating system (most of those that have a keyboard do, but so do some other models), then you may not have to buy a dedicated MP3 player to listen to your MP3 files. If you go to **www.utopiasoft.com**, you can download a trial version of a program called Hum, which will allow Windows CE-based palmtops to recognize and then play MP3 songs. The results are a bit rough and ready, but perfectly acceptable.

MUSIC AND PORTABLE PCS

There's nothing to stop you from playing back MP3 music on a suitably equipped portable PC. You simply need to make sure that it has either a pair of built-in speakers or a headphone socket. Obviously, you also need a way of getting the music on to the portable PC in the first place. The best way is to download MP3 music directly from the Internet, using the built-in modem if your computer has one, or an external modem if not.

DRESSING UP SONIQUE

Sonique is one of a new generation of PC programs that ignore
Windows' design conventions by using a technique called
"skinning." The results can be innovative and exciting.

DOWNLOADING SKINS

One of the many distinctive features of
Sonique, our chosen MP3 player, is that
you can "dress it up" to make it look and
feel different – even to the extent of
adding special visual effects. Here's how
to make it all work.

1 FINDING A SKIN

● Sonique uses "skins" to
change its appearance. You
can download them for free
by going to the Sonique
Internet site. Launch your
web browser in the usual
way and type in
www.sonique.com in the
Address line.

● Look on the opening
page and find the section
called **Top Ten Skins**. This
is a list of the most popular
"looks" for Sonique at any
given time. Obviously, the
names will change over
time, so just pick one and
click on it.

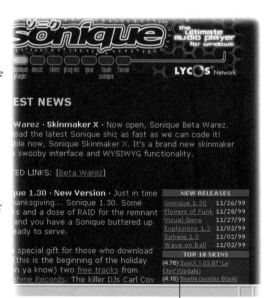

Top Ten Skins ●

● You'll be taken to the page containing your chosen skin. Here, you'll see a preview so that you can decide whether or not you like the look of it before downloading. Remember that Sonique has three distinct onscreen views. Typically you'll see the skin displayed in the large and medium-sized views as these are the two that demonstrate the greatest visual differences.

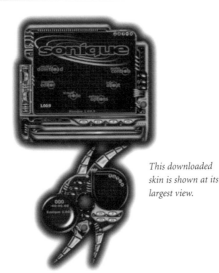

This downloaded skin is shown at its largest view.

● If you like the skin, scroll down toward the bottom of the screen and click on the **download skin** option.

2 DOWNLOADING THE SKIN

● If you don't like the skin, check out the alternatives in other categories, which you'll find on the website. In each case, you'll be able to see a preview of the skin before you decide to download it. We've chosen one called **Katharsis** and clicked **download skin**.

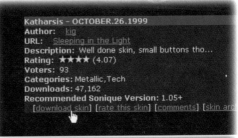

● In the **File Download** dialog box, Windows asks if you want to download the file and save it to disk. Click on the **OK** button.

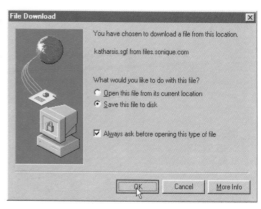

3 COPYING THE SKIN FILE

● Windows then asks where you'd like to copy the file on your hard disk. Ours is going to the Windows desktop where it's easy to find. You can always move it later on.

● The file is now downloaded to your computer.

Sonique's three views
Remember that Sonique has three distinct sizes, depending on how big your screen is, how many programs you have loaded, etc. Once you've downloaded and installed a skin, the look of each of the three views automatically alters.

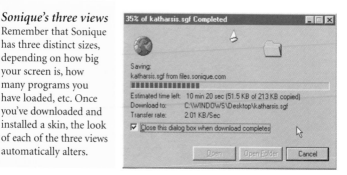

INSTALLING THE SKIN

Downloading the skin to change the way that Sonique looks is only the first step toward personalizing the program. After installation, you need to use Sonique's program's setup options to complete the "skinning" process.

1 INSTALLING THE SKIN

● The Katharsis skin is safely on your hard disk. Now you need to go and find it. When you have found it, click on it once with the right mouse button and then choose **Install into Sonique** from the pop-up menu.
● At first, it looks as though nothing has happened, so click on Sonique's **setup options**.

CUSTOMIZING OTHER PROGRAMS

There are many different programs you can customize like this, using freely available skins. Two of the best Internet sites for sources of skins are:
www.customize.org and **www.skinz.org**. You'll find details of the programs that can be skinned and the skins to go with them.

• *Setup Options*

● When the next screen appears, click on the **Skins** option, toward the right of Sonique's central display. Make sure that the General tab has been selected first.

Click on the Skins option ●

● Next, click on the large up arrow and you'll notice that the preview in the middle of the screen changes to reflect the newly installed skin.

Click on the up arrow ●

Switch skins
You can download and install as many skins as you like in exactly the same way. Switch between them whenever you like using the procedures described in this section. It's like having a new program every day of the week.

● Finally, click anywhere
on the preview image with
the right mouse button
and, after a short delay,
your new skin will appear.

VISUAL ADD-INS

Sonique's visual wardrobe is extensive, but
it doesn't stop with skins. You can also run
the program in an unusual visual mode,
which allows you to watch special effects,
such as psychedelic light-shows that throb
and pulse in time to the music.

1 GOING TO VISUAL MODE

● To check out Sonique's
visual mode, make sure
that you have a song loaded
and then, from the main
screen, click on the **visual
mode** option.

● Click on the play button and watch the screen in the middle of Sonique. You should see a psychedelic light show.

● If you don't, it could be because you do not have a visual add-in loaded. As the music plays, click on the large up arrow to cycle through the four effects that come with the program. Below is the **Spectrum** 1.0 add-in.

The Spectrum visual effect moves in time with the music

Use the up arrow to scroll through the visual effects

KEEPING UP-TO-DATE

Most good sites offer a free newsletter sent out as an email. Simply fill in a form on the website, giving them your email address. This will save you from having to keep going back to a particular site to see what has changed.

● Now we'll find a new visual add-in from the Internet. Launch your browser and go to the Sonique website (**www.sonique.com**). When you get there, scroll down to the bottom of the page and click on the **vis plug-ins archive** option.

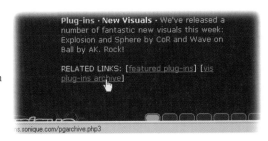

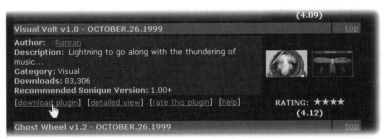

● On the next page, check out the small images of the various visual plug-ins available and pick one you like. The one we've chosen is called **Visual Volt**. Click the **download plugin** option, and download the file as before.

● When it has downloaded, disconnect from the Internet and close your browser. Find the Volt icon and double-click on it. It installs instantly and then displays a screen of technical information. Simply close this by clicking on the **x** in the top right-hand corner.

● Check out your new visual plug-in by loading Sonique. Then click on the **Visual Mode** option. Make sure you have a song loaded, then click the play button.

● If you don't see anything happen, click on the upward-pointing arrow until the small screen in the center of Sonique displays your chosen special effect.This is how **Visual Volt** appears.

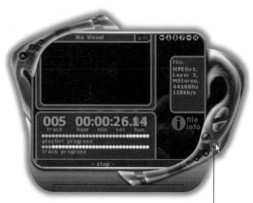

Play button ●

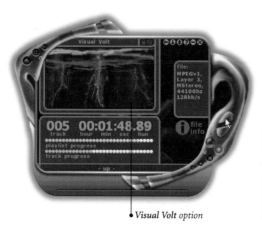

Opposite page
There are so many skins available through Sonique's website that it would be impossible to show them all. From top to bottom; Antiskin, Fluid Skin, and Nautilus.

● *Visual Volt option*

YES, BUT CAN I READ IT?

With the wealth of visual add-ins available for programs such as Sonique, it's extremely easy to get carried away and end up with something that looks fantastic, but is actually rather hard to use. Some skin designers forget that people actually have to use the skins, and they put so much effort into making their designs exciting and artistic that they mistakenly make the buttons too small, hard to see, or even unusable.

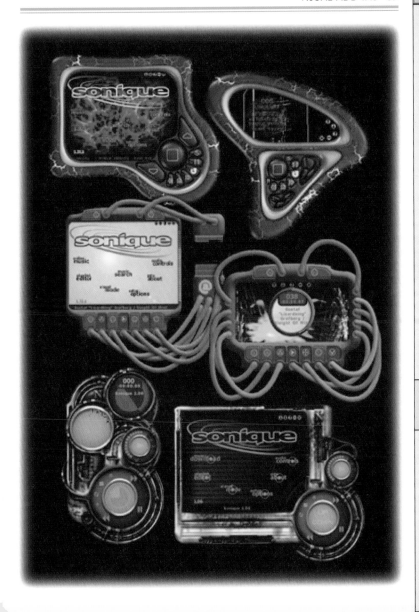

GLOSSARY

BROWSER
Sometimes called a web browser. This is a program that allows your computer to display websites stored on the Internet with all their text, pictures, and sounds. Browsers provide ways of storing favorite sites so that you can easily revisit them later, let you download files (copy them from the Internet to your computer), and join Internet chat rooms.

CD-R
A kind of CD-ROM drive and disc, which you can use for recording – much like a floppy disk. The difference is that you can only record onto a CD-R disc once.

CD-RW
Another specialized form of CD-ROM. Very similar to CD-R discs and drives, except that you can record data onto them repeatedly.

COPY
To make an exact copy of a sound, document, or selection of text that already exists elsewhere – either on your computer or on the Internet. Making a copy of something does not disturb or alter the original in any way.

DIALOG BOX
A panel that is displayed on screen and allows you to specify particular options and switch functions on and off by clicking on them using the mouse.

DOCKING STATION
A cradle, permanently connected to a computer, into which you plug a smaller device so that it can communicate with the PC.

DOWNLOAD
To copy software from a website contained on a remote computer down onto your hard drive.

DVD
Stands for digital versatile disc. A kind of souped-up CD-ROM that can store many times more information and offers superior sound and pictures.

MIDI FILE
A collection of instructions that tells the electronic instruments on your sound card what to play and when – including when to start and stop, which notes to play, and at what volume.

MODEM
A device that connects your computer to the Internet. It plugs into the telephone line.

MP3
The so-called audio "layer" of MPEG. It is a way of storing digital sound that will play back at almost CD quality while taking up very little space.

MPEG
The Motion Picture Experts Group, an international body that tries to improve and standardize the way video is stored and displayed on computers.

PLUG-IN
A program that adds features to

a web browser so that it can handle, for example, 3D and multimedia files.

REAL AUDIO
A way of storing music on the Internet and then playing it back from there, instead of making you download the music first before you can play it. Real Audio music is never downloaded to your computer.

WAV FILE
By default, the format Windows uses for digital audio, such as the sound you hear when Windows starts.

WEB ADDRESS
Just like houses, websites have to have a unique address so that you can locate them.

WEBSITE
Websites are made up of individual web pages and are like electronic magazine pages with text and pictures and links that can take you to other web pages.

WINDOWS
The operating system that runs on most home computers. It handles the communications between the "brains" of the computer and the software, the filing system, and the peripheral components such as the display, keyboard, mouse, printer, scanner and modem.

WINDOWS CE
The version of Windows designed for palmtop-sized, battery-powered, portable computers.

INDEX

ACKNOWLEDGMENTS

PUBLISHER'S ACKNOWLEDGMENTS
Dorling Kindersley would like to thank the following:
Paul Mattock of APM, Brighton, for commissioned photography.
Microsoft Corporation for permission to reproduce screens
from within Microsoft® Internet Explorer.
mp3.com, shawncolvin.com/sonymusic.com, sonique.com,
stereophonics.co.uk (octweb.com), take5.real.com,
ubl.com (artistdirect.com), winamp.com (nullsoft.com)

*Every effort has been made to trace the copyright holders.
The publisher apologizes for any unintentional omissions and would be pleased,
in such cases, to place an acknowledgment in future editions of this book.*

Microsoft is a registered trademark of Microsoft Corporation
in the United States and/or other countries.